Creative Writing

Prompts and Exercises to Boost Creativity, Beat
Writer's Block, and Develop Craft

MARIE EAGER

ISBN-13: 978-0692286555
ISBN-10: 0692286551

Web Address: www.HowToWriteNow.com
Cover Design: SelfPubBookCovers.com/daringnovelist

Contents

Introduction

Struggling with writers block is a pitfall that most writers will face more than once. Writing prompts have long been used as a tool to help get the creative juices flowing and unlock the doors of imagination. This book is no exception. Designed with the storyteller in mind, each section contains a carefully selected blend of activities to boost creativity, beat writer's block, and hone craft.

The book is divided into four key areas. You will activate your imagination and develop creative problem solving skills as you explore Character, Setting, Plot, and Voice. As you move through the pages you will find activities ranging from open-ended prompts to specific creative strategies.

The prompts and exercises in this book are intended to be completed in 15 minutes or less. Some have been divided into two parts, A and B, so that they can be broken up over two days in case you want to spend more time on one part. Activities are grouped by focus: Character, Setting, Plot, or Voice. Within each section, exercises that build on each other can be found either consecutively or spread out amongst other exercises. This has been done in order to give you a fresher perspective when you return to the original piece of writing.

How To Use This Book

As every writer has a unique voice and creative process, none of the strategies explored in this book will work for all writers all of the time. Rather, each writer is encouraged to explore their own creative and writing processes. Don't be afraid to try new techniques, but also don't be afraid to set them aside if they don't resonate. Add what works well to your personal toolkit. Treat the rest as an exploration.

There are a couple of important things to remember as you progress through the material. First, save your work! Some of the exercises build upon each other, so you'll want to keep a file of your work handy for reference. Second, activities can be completed consecutively, randomly, by topic, by following threads of related exercises, or all of the above. Simply refer to the table of contents if you want to skip around. Engage with the material in whatever way works best for you.

And finally, relax and have fun! Enjoy the journey. There are no right or wrong answers. Each prompt or exercise, each question or reflection, is simply an opportunity to explore. I hope that as you work through the pages you will find yourself engaging with your own creativity in new and exciting ways, and that by doing so, your love of writing will continue to expand.

Best Wishes,
Marie Eager

Character

Character 1

A) Choose a person, real or imaginary. It might be you, someone you know, a famous or historical figure, a fictional character, or even a character that you have created. List 10 words or phrases in each of the following categories about this person's personality:

•Strengths
•Weaknesses
•Fears
•Braveries
•Quirks

B) Choose one item from each of the five lists. Answer the following questions about the qualities you chose:

•What past experience or group of experiences might have contributed to this aspect of their personality?
•In what way is this aspect of their personality a strength, weakness, fear, bravery, or quirk?
•Could this quality be categorized in more than one way? How so?
•How might this quality affect the way in which this person forms relationships with others?
•How might this quality affect this person's ability to reach goals?
•How might this quality be useful?
•How might it be detrimental?

Future Exercises: Character 7, 16

Character 2

A) Your character has an unusually heightened sense of smell. Write a brief narrative taking him through an ordinary day, starting from the moment he wakes up. Take this heightened sense into account as your character experiences his daily life. Before you begin, take a moment to jot down the answers to the following questions:

•How does his sensitivity affect his living arrangements?
•How does it affect the way in which he views and experiences the world around him?
•Is it distracting, or has he learned to handle it? How so?
•In what ways is this sense useful? Inconvenient? Annoying? Pleasurable?
•Is he aware that his ability to smell is stronger than most? How does this knowledge (or lack of knowledge) affect the way he views himself and others?

B) Once you've finished your story, go back through the list of questions. Did the writing process deepen or change any of your answers? How so?

Future Exercises: Character 15

Character 3

A) Spend 7-10 minutes free-writing a break-up scene. The only information you have to begin with is this:

•The participants are Marlo and Jenny.
•Marlo is tall and thin with black hair.
•Jenny loves parakeets but is allergic to them.

B) Rather than taking time to think about further Character for Marlo and Jenny, simply begin writing. Remember, this is a free-write. Let the scene unfold as you write it. After you finish writing, answer the following questions:

•How did the characters' personalities and motivations come out during the free-writing process?
•Did you have a visual image of your characters in your mind from the beginning or did it develop over time?
•Did your sense of empathy with your characters increase as you wrote? Why or why not?
•What did you like and/or dislike about free-writing as a tool for Character?

Character 4

A) Brainstorm a list of characteristics that you might associate with each of the following:

•A Thief
•A Child
•A Businessman
•A Musician
•A Soldier
•A Scientist

B) For each, include 10 traits that you would consider stereotypical and 10 that you would consider unusual. Consider whether the stereotypical traits are generally justified and whether the unusual traits are believable.

Character 5

It's the age-old story: Teenager from small town feels like life is going nowhere. Discovers that he/she has been endowed with superpowers. Proceeds to save the city/country/world/universe, often while wearing theatrical disguises.

This time, *you* are the teenager. After 17 years living a fairly mundane life, you discover that you have a super power. Answer the following questions:

•What super power would you choose?
•Why did you choose this?
•Are there any limitations on this power?
•What would you do with it?
•Would you tell others of your ability? Why or why not?
•How would this power benefit your life?
•How would this power complicate your life?

Future Exercises: Character 8

Character 6

Choose a familiar tale and rewrite 1-2 scenes from the point of view of a secondary character who is not the antagonist. Focus on Character. As you write, consider the following questions:

•What makes us care about this person?
•How might his or her personality affect the actions that they take?
•How will this person's participation in events affect him or her tomorrow? Next week? Next year?
•Would the story events have unfolded different if this person were absent? Why or why not?

Character 7

A) Time to pull *Character 1* back out of the drawer. Remember when we made a list of qualities relating to the personality of a character? Let's take it a step further. Review what you wrote for the first exercise. Considering the characteristics that you explored, what kinds of habits might this person have developed? Make a list of 5-10 habits and/or mannerisms stemming from this person's personality.

B) After you've finished, choose one and answer the following questions:

•Would you consider this a good habit, a bad habit, both, or neither?
•Is the character aware of this habit?
•Is the character aware of where this aspect comes from?
•If they are aware, how do they feel about it?
•What about their current behavior or circumstances perpetuates this habit?

Future Exercises: Character 16, 21

Character 8

A) Remember the super power you wrote about in *Character 5*? Take a moment to review your writing and then create a character inspired by your answers. Write a scene around the first time that your character discovered that he or she had a special ability. This discovery is a completely unexpected event. As the scene unfolds, try to create a solid sense of what the character is experiencing viscerally as they use their super power for the first time. Include all five senses. Also include your character's reactions to the sensations of the experience.

B) After completing the scene, read back through it and answer the following questions:

•What sensory details did you include?
•How did those sensory details give us a sense of the character's mental and emotional state?
•Do you feel that including sensory details made the character seem more real? Why or why not?
•What would it take to make

Character 9

A) If you're in the habit of doing your writing exercises in the same place every time, try to put yourself in a new setting for this one. It can be as simple as moving to a different room in the house, sitting outside, or taking a 'writing break' while you're out shopping or at work. For five minutes, notice what sensory input you are receiving and write down as many sensations as you can. Make sure to hit all five senses.

B) For the next five minutes, delve into the mind of a character that you have been working on or that you've enjoyed reading about in the past. For each sensation you took note of, write down how this person would react to it. Does he wrinkle his nose at the scent of lilacs, or breathe deeply to draw it in? Would she smile at the sound of children playing or roll her eyes in annoyance?

Rather than simply listing reactions, try to write from your character's point of view.

Character 10

A) Start with a name. Write it at the top of your paper. Brainstorm a list of questions about this person. For example:

- •Who are they?
- •Where are they from?
- •What general attitudes do they have?
- •What is their current life situation?
- •How did they get to where they are now?
- •What are their goals and motivations?
- •Do they have friends? Family?
- •What role do those people play in your character's life?

B) After coming up with at least 10 questions, go back and answer the first few in 1-2 sentences each. Do your answers raise any new questions? If so, write them down. Repeat the process until you have a list of at least 25 questions about your character. Don't worry about answering all of them, but do hang on to your list for future reference.

Future Exercises: Character 13, 18

Character 11

Choose the villain from a familiar tale. Generate a backstory from him or her. Give them at least one page of writing. Here are some questions to get you started:

•Where did this person come from?
•What was this person's life like when they were a child?
•What have been the most difficult elements of this person's life so far? The most beautiful?
•What makes this person a villain?
•What are his or her goals and motivations? Where do they come from?
•Where was this person one year ago? Five? Ten?

Future Exercises: Character 22

Character 12

A) Estrella woke up this morning to discover that everyone in the world had vanished. Write a one-page story about what happens next.

B) Read back through your writing and answer the following questions:

•How did Estrella's character come out as you wrote?
•How did extraordinary circumstances affect her?
•How did her reactions to the situation demonstrate Estrella's personality, beliefs, and motivations?

Character 13

For this exercise you'll need the list of character questions you generated in *Character 10*. Go back through your list and answer the questions. You might choose to answer some questions in just a sentence or two, and others over several paragraphs or pages. Do as many as you can in fifteen minutes, but don't rush. Take your time and really get to know your character.

As you answer the questions, further questions might come to mind. Continue to make note of these you go through the list.

Future Exercises: Character 18

Character 14

Respond to the following prompt:

Melanie wasn't sure why everyone was looking at her. The room had fallen silent as soon as she walked in, and now six pairs of eyes focused on her face, watching. She shifted her weight uncomfortably. Where was one supposed to look at times like these?

Character 15

Write a scene involving a Musician, a Caretaker, and a Thief.

Character 16

It's once again time to pull *Character 1* and *Character 7* out of the drawer. For the following prompt, assume that the main character has one or more of the personality traits that you've been analyzing in earlier exercises. After reading the prompt, finish the scene. Make sure that whatever your character does to resolve the situation, the personality trait you've been analyzing plays a critical role in your character's behavior. Show this aspect of their personality through speech, mannerisms, facial expressions, tone of voice, dialogue—whatever you feel works best in making your character real.

The sandwich looked terrible. Wilted lettuce hung out the back, visibly brown on the edges. I'd asked for no ketchup but there it was, escaping from between the soggy crusts like blood from an oozing wound. The kid working behind the counter had left visible finger indentations in the bread when he threw the thing together. He watched me now with thin lips drawn into a straight line. Daring me to take exception.

Future Exercises: Character 17

Character 17

Let's take *Character 16* a step farther. Spend no more than two minutes jotting down some basic background and character traits for the boy who made the sandwich. When you finish, rewrite your entire scene from the boy's point of view. After you finish, ask yourself the following questions:

•How did the personalities of your two characters affect their interaction?
•Was the outcome of the situation dependent on the personal characteristics of your characters?
•How might the scene have played out differently with different personality types?

Future Exercises: Character 21

Character 18

A) Remember the questions you've been asking and answering in *Character 10* and *Character 13*? By now you should have the start of a fairly well-rounded character. Even if you haven't answered all of the questions yet, the asking process itself has hopefully given you some feel for who your character is.

For this exercise, write a scene in which your character has an unexpected encounter with an old acquaintance.

B) After writing the scene, consider the following questions:

•How did your character react to the acquaintance?
•How will the encounter affect her or him going forward, or will it?
•As you wrote the encounter, did it bring up any new questions for you about the character?
•How about after you'd finished?
•Did you find the answers simply by asking these questions, or are you still wondering?

Character 19

Write a first contact scene. This may be first contact between individuals, communities, cultures, even aliens. Whatever you choose, make sure that the two parties do not share the same background. As you write consider the following questions:

•In what ways might differences in background affect the way that your characters view themselves and each other?
•How might differences in motivation affect the way that your characters approach the meeting?
•How might the outcome have been different if those involved had shared the same background?

Character 20

You are an android recently freed from a life time of servitude. On the day of your liberation, a machine rights group provided you with an advocate to make sure that the process went smoothly. Now that everything has been taken care of, the advocate pressures you to help the group with certain dubious activities. When you decline, she implies that you owe them. What happens next?

Character 21

A) For this exercise you will need to bring out your story from *Character 16*. Read through the scene once to refresh it in your memory.

Go back through the story and remove all adjectives, adverbs, and descriptive phrases that relate to the main character. Re-read the story. Ask yourself:

•How did removing these words change your perspective of the character?
•Did removing these words change the tone of the writing? How so?

B) Go through the story once more. This time, choose a personality trait at random. Put the descriptive language back in, but try using different words to reflect the personality trait you've chosen. Re-read the story. Ask yourself:

•How did the new language change your perspective of the character?
•Did the solution still make sense with the new personality trait?
•If yes, how could you make the original characteristic more integral?
•In no, how could you change the story to make the new characteristic more integral?

Character 22

Take a look at the backstory you generated for your villain in *Character 11*. Choose one element from the backstory. Write about how that element contributed to your character's current state of villainy.

,

Character 23

In this exercises you will come up with a character and develop him or her one line at a time. Start with the general and become more and more specific with each step. For example:

•A girl.
•She is living in the 1920s in Paris.
•She lives in Paris with her parents, a housekeeper named Rebecca, and a dog that everyone has forgotten about.
•She is the youngest person in the house, with dark hair, bright eyes, and a continual craving for sharp cheese.
•Life at home is not what it once was. There are too many closed doors and hushed voices and not enough escapades. It all makes her want to scream, but she keeps quiet because keeping quiet is the only way she can help.

Future Exercises: Character 24

Character 24

Review your writing from *Character 23*. Answer the following questions:

•As you explored your character, what directions did the exercise take you in?
•What kinds of details did you come up with? Did you write about your character's psyche, life situation, goals, likes and dislikes?
•How specific did you get?
•As you wrote, did ideas for stories occur to you?
•How long did it take you to get a sense of your character's background?
•If you were to meet this character in real life, would you like them? Why or why not?
•If you were to use this character in future writing, what kinds of stories would he or she fit into?

Character 25

Respond to the following prompt. Focus on establishing character:

Thirteen ducks she'd asked for, and like a fool he'd agreed.

Setting

Setting 1

Write a description of your surroundings. Pay attention not only to what you see, but to what you smell, hear, feel, etc. Write for at least 10 minutes. In that time you might choose to capture everything around you on the page or to focus on just one aspect of your surroundings. Either way, go deep. Help us feel what it's like to be where you are at the moment of your writing.

Future Exercises: Setting 2, 3

Setting 2

A) Spend five minutes listing as many things as you can from your surroundings. Don't just write down what you see, write down what you hear, smell, etc.

B) Once you've finished, spend another five minutes turning your list into a narrative description of your surroundings.

C) Think back to the *Setting 1* exercise. Ask yourself the following questions:

•How did making a list before I wrote help or hinder the flow of my writing?
•Did I include more or fewer details in my description this time?
•Was the quality of my description affected by making a list before hand?
•Was it easier or more difficult to write a narrative description after making a list as opposed to starting from scratch?

Tip: Remember, there are no wrong or right answers to these questions. They are simply meant to help you understand your preferences as a writer and get a feel for your own creative flow.

Future Exercises: Setting 3

Setting 3

Choose one of the descriptions that you wrote in either *Setting 1* or *Setting 2*. Describe the setting again, from the point of view of a person. This time, the focus is on showing rather than telling. Communicate the setting to the reader through the character's actions, words, and reactions. Avoid relying on narrative description.

Setting 4

You have just been released from a 10 year prison sentence. Write what happens next, focusing on how the outside world might feel to you after a 10 year absence. Consider the following:

•What did you miss while you were in prison?
•What did you forget about?
•How might technology have changed?
•What every day sounds haven't you heard in 10 years?
•What is likely to have stayed the same?

Setting 5

Think of the last book or story you read. Make a quick list of the kinds of settings that appeared, as best as you can remember them. Answer the following questions:

•How many different settings did you remember?
•Did setting have any impact on the actions of the characters?
•Did setting play a role in the outcome of the story? How so?
•In what ways did the author make the setting feel real or grounded?
•Are there any specific details of a setting which stuck with you?
•Did you have a clear visual sense of the setting when you were reading?

Setting 6

Respond to the following prompt, with a focus on establishing setting:

Mr. Williams can speak with trees. No one else in the neighborhood realizes this except little Joey Kingsly.

Future Exercise: Setting 20

Setting 7

Think about your favorite place on Earth. If you don't have one, think of a place that has significance for you. In one page, describe the setting. Consider the following questions as you write:

•Why is this place important to you?

•Have you been to this place more than once?

•If so, has this place changed over time or remained pretty much the same?

•What are the physical details of the setting?

•What are the sensory details?

•What emotions are evoked when you think of this place?

•If this place is important to you because of events that occurred there, then how did the setting influence events?

•If you could never see this place again, what would you miss most about it?

•Does this place have a functional purpose it? What is it?

Setting 8

What kinds of words do you associate with different kinds of places? For each of the following places, write a paragraph describing how you feel when you think about that place. Try not to rely on stereotypes unless they represent how you really feel.

•a cemetery
•a shopping mall
•a museum
•the inside of an airplane
•a forest

Setting 9

Describe your dream home with either words, a drawing, or both. Include layout, architectural features, landscaping, home systems, décor, furnishings, and the purpose of each room. Be as detailed as possible.

Future Exercises: Setting 10

Setting 10

Look over your description of your dream home from *Setting 9*. Answer the following questions:

•Why do I want this house?
•What about this house excites me?
•How would I feel actually living in this house?
•How would others feel in this house, such as family, friends, and acquaintances?
•How can design elements such as layout and décor affect the emotional tone of a space?
•If I lived in this house, how would the physical aspects of the home affect my day to day life?

Setting 11

Respond to the following prompt with a focus on setting:

The first person to step out of the car was Phil. He kept his mouth closed, trying to look normal as he filtered the air through his nostrils. The next one out was Carey. The poor kid's eyes were already watering.

Setting 12

A) Choose any story that you have written for another prompt. Add five details to the setting. Also add five sensory responses that your character has to his or her surroundings. The two sets of details don't necessarily have to be related.

B) Read back through your work. Answer the following questions:

•How does adding details to the setting affect the piece as a whole?
•How does adding sensory responses affect our understanding of the setting?
•Did the extra details expand the story or make it feel encumbered?
•If you were to edit this story, which details would keep? Why?
•If you were to edit this story, which details would you throw out? Why?

Setting 13

Write a scene in which the setting is also one of the characters.

Setting 14

Respond to the following prompt with a focus on setting:

Mick's dog was the ugliest thing I'd ever seen. She was such a sweetheart that you didn't notice it at first, and by the time you did you were so in love with her that you'd slap anyone who said she was less than beautiful.

As you write, include the following details in your setting:

•temperature
•color
•smell
•sound
•texture
•vibration
•light
•objects

Setting 15

For 10 minutes write an event that takes place on a farm. It can be any kind of farm—animals, crops, silk worms, even people—but the farm must be integral to the story.

Setting 16

A) Choose a specific place, such as a room, a park, or a school. Write a paragraph describing the setting. Set the tone as light-hearted or happy. Answer the following questions:

•How can setting contribute to the emotional tone of a piece of writing?
•What kinds of words did you use to create your tone?
•Did you find yourself anthropomorphizing aspects of the setting in order to accomplish the task?
•If so, how might you make a place feel 'light hearted' or 'happy' without anthropomorphizing?

B) Now write a new paragraph describing the same place. This time, make the place appear grim. Repeat the exercise again, experimenting with different emotional tones. Do not change anything in the setting itself; rather, change the way in which you choose to describe it.

Future Exercises: Setting 19

Setting 17

How many different ways can you think of to describe the sun on your face? Come up with at least 10 examples.

Setting 18

Respond to the following prompt.

There was just too much to get done. Dave put his head in his hands. He felt like his brain was about to explode.

Setting 19

A) Review the work you did for *Setting 16*. Choose one of the emotional tones you explored and write a new paragraph in your chosen setting. This time, insert two people into the setting. Give the paragraph the same emotional tone but show that tone through your characters' actions rather than through description of the setting.

B) Rewrite the paragraph again but this time establish the tone through dialogue.

Setting 20

Pull out the writing you did in *Setting 6*. Re-write your story in a completely different setting. For example, if your original story took place in a suburban neighborhood in the 1970s, this time let it take place in future times in a technologically advanced high-rise apartment complex.

Setting 21

A) In 60 seconds write down everything you can about your surroundings.

B) After you've finished, write a story that uses each of the items you wrote down.

Setting 22

Free-write a story on any topic. The setting for this story must contain the following elements:

•a creaky door
•the night sky
•a tunnel
•a weeping willow
•a spring
•parrots

Setting 23

Respond to the following prompt:

Shannon blinked under a sun riding high overhead. A breeze touched her face but she couldn't tell where it came from. The leaves on the trees were so still they might have been painted. She licked a finger. Offered it to the air. Nothing.

Setting 24

Write a story set in a landscape that your main character hates. Perhaps she hates snow and is living in Norway, or can't stand to be hot but is stuck in the Sonoran Desert. Help us to really see the setting through the character's eyes. Remember the following as you write:

•Use all five senses.
•Do more than just describe—reveal the surroundings to the reader through the character's thoughts and actions.
•Set an emotional landscape as well as a physical one.

Future Exercises: Setting 25

Setting 25

Bring out your story from *Setting 24*. Rewrite the story in the same setting but this time your character feels a deep sense of warmth and connection towards his or her surroundings. After writing, read back through your work and consider the following:

•In order to accomplish the task, did you change words related to the character, the setting, or both?

•How might word choice affect a reader's interpretation of a scene?

•If you were to continue working on this story, would you work from the version wherein the character liked or disliked the surroundings? Why?

•How does a clear setting contribute to a firmly grounded character?

Plot

Plot 1

Dan is a 43 year-old single father of two children. He has a job in investment banking that keeps him mildly entertained but is not particularly rewarding. He takes the most joy out of life by taking his children on 'adventures' in the nearby national forest.

This afternoon Dan drove his kids into the park for a weekend of camping, river rafting, and general family togetherness. He is just reeling in a couple of fish for dinner when one of the kids comes to tell him that the youngest is stuck in a tree, afraid to climb down. Dan must get from the river bank to the tree and bring down his frightened son before it gets dark.

The initial task is straightforward; Dan follows the older child to the tree, climbs up, and comes down with his child. Consider, however, what other obstacles could be in his path. These additional obstacles will be the focus of this exercise.

Create four columns on your paper. In the first, make a list of five obstacles Dan might face in reaching his goal. In the second column, write down one way that Dan might overcome each obstacle as he progresses towards rescuing his son. In the third column, write down how Dan's attempted solution for each obstacle might fail. In the fourth, write down ways that Dan's failures might actually bring him closer to his goal in some way.

Future Exercises: Plot 9

Plot 2

A) Brainstorm a list of 25 one line story openings.

B) Choose one of your story openings and craft an opening paragraph.

Plot 3

A) Respond to the following prompt by free-writing a 1-2 page story:

Aaron frowned, a strange tilt to his lower lip that always made people uncomfortable.

B) After you finish, take a moment to analyze your story. Answer the following questions:

- Is there any structure to your story?
- Did a clear beginning, middle, and end come out?
- Was there a problem to be solved or a goal to be met?
- Was there a protagonist? An antagonist?
- Does the writing rely more on setting dialogue, action, or Character?
- Did any of your characters interact with their environment?
- Did objects come into play?

Remember there are no right or wrong answers! This is just an opportunity to think about what kinds of story elements came out naturally during your free-write.

Plot 4

Free-write a story around the following prompt:

Janet had never felt so good in her life. There were a hundred things she'd been planning to do at the office today, but none of them mattered. All she wanted was to lie on her back in the courtyard in her $3000 pantsuit and let the grass mess up her hair. It wasn't every day that one found out the world was going to end, and she intended to enjoy it.

Plot 5

Write a scene involving the following:

•a mermaid
•a robot
•a politician
•a pair of geese

Plot 6

A) Describe, step by step, how to cook your favorite food.

B) Write a first-person narration of someone trying to cook this recipe. For every step, give your character a problem to overcome.

Plot 7

The following is an ending. Write the story leading up to it.

Jack grinned. Lacie shook her head and continued stitching up his arm with quick, methodical strokes. After everything they'd been through, she supposed she should be smiling too.

"Come on, Lace," Jack said, cocking his head to one side. The corners of his mouth stayed up, but some of the exhaustion had crept back into the lines of his face. He wanted her to be okay, she could see it in the tightness around his eyes and the way they flickered, just once. He wanted them both to be okay.

And maybe they were. Lacie looked past him at the devastation that surrounded them. It had always been like this for and Jack. They lived, and everyone else died. If nothing else, at least they would get to keep trying. She allowed herself a brief smile. Jack reached out with his good arm and caressed her cheek with the back of his hand. "We'll get it right next time," he said.

Lacie nodded. Perhaps they would.

Plot 8

A yellow retriever is sniffing around in the crawlspace of an abandoned house. His owner, a balding man in his late fifties, is standing on the weathered porch trying to pick up a shred of signal on his cell phone. An old ice-cream truck is rusting in the field across the way. The sound of an engine can be heard in the distance, getting closer. What happens next?

Plot 9

A) Bring out the work you did for *Plot 1*. Using your notes, make an outline for a sequence of events. Start with Dan fishing on the river bank. Include at least of three of the obstacles that you identified, including their attempted solutions and failures. They can occur in any order but should logically connect.

B) Create a final obstacle that Dan overcomes successfully. The solution to this obstacle has one stipulation: It must be influenced, directly or indirectly, by Dan's earlier failures. This influence should be such that the outcome could not have occurred if Dan had not earlier tried and failed to overcome the other obstacles. For example, perhaps the solution is made possible by what Dan learned from his previous failures, or perhaps his previous failures motivated him to try something new that he would otherwise not have considered.

Plot 10

Think about fairy tale adaptations that you've read or seen in the movies. How have the creators adapted familiar tales? Did they set it in modern times? Work from the point of view of a different character? Add a twist?

Choose a fairy tale you like. Spend 10-15 minutes retelling the story so that it is set in modern times. The choice is yours. Don't worry about trying to write the entire story in just 15 minutes. Simply start at whatever point in the story you choose and write for the full amount of time. As you work, consider the following questions:

•Are there any significant plot elements that you would need to change to make the story reasonable in a modern setting?
•How would modern technology, law, and sociality affect the course of events?
•What would be the impact of story events on the surrounding world?
•What kinds of lives would the characters' have if they grew up in today's world?

Plot 11

Think about a character that you have either created, are thinking about creating, or have enjoyed reading. Divide your paper into four columns. In the first column, write down a list of goals that this character might have. These might be situational goals, life goals, interpersonal goals, etc. In the second, write down a situational challenge that your character might face in trying to reach these goals. In the third, write down a psychological challenge for each goal. In the final column, describe a stake for each goal—something that will be lost if the character doesn't reach the goal.

Future Exercises: Plot 12

Plot 12

Pull out your work from *Plot 13*. Choose one set of goals/challenges/stakes and use them as a prompt for today's writing. Make sure to write for at least 10 minutes.

Plot 13

A) Imagine that you can enter the dreams of others. Answer the following:

•How would this ability be useful to you?
•How would it be detrimental?
•What ethical considerations might this ability bring up?
•What would the world be like if everyone had this ability?
•What would the world be like if only some people had this ability?
•What would the world be like if corporations, governments, or other groups could control who had this ability?

B) Brainstorm a list of story ideas incorporating this ability. Limit each idea to three sentences.

Future Exercise: Plot 14

Plot 14

A) Take a look at the list of story ideas you generated for *Plot 13*. Choose one story idea from your list. Expand it into a brief outline for a 1-2 page short story.

B) After you've finished your outline, spend your remaining time free-writing backstory.

Future Exercises: Plot 15

Plot 15

A) Review the outline you created in *Plot 14*. Spend 10-12 minutes writing the opening paragraphs.

B) As you wrote, did you think of any new ideas for your story? If so, incorporate them into your outline.

Plot 16

A) Make a list of 10 free-standing titles for novels, short stories, essays, or poems. Choose three and write an opening paragraph for each.

B) As you wrote the opening paragraphs, did ideas for further story development come to mind? Did you think of problems, settings, or characters? Jot down any thoughts you have.

Plot 17

Choose any scene that you have written for a past exercise. Write an alternate ending that shakes everything up. If your protagonist won, make him lose, if love was thwarted, let it thrive, if the bad guy cried, make him laugh. You must find a way to make your new ending a believable extension of what comes before it.

Plot 18

A) The following sentence will be the geographical 'middle' of your piece:
Martin looked down and realized the street had gone out from under him.

Write the sentence on the middle line of your paper. Expand the story in both directions, writing one line before and one line after until you've filled at least one page.

B) Consider the following questions:

• What did you learn from this exercise?
• How was this experience the same or different from other methods of story generation that you've tried?
• Did you find this method helpful? Why or why not?
• Do you think this method would be useful for generating ideas, writing stories, both, or neither?

Plot 19

Think back to a crucial crossroads in your life, a time when you made a decision that changed the direction of your journey. It doesn't have to be a good vs. bad crossroads, but it should be a distinct point in time when a single decision affected everything that has followed. Examples might be moving to a new state, choosing what to study in school, turning down or accepting a marriage proposal, etc.

For 10 minutes, write down an alternate version of events. Consider the following:

•What would have happened if you had gone the other direction?
•What events might have occurred in the weeks that followed? The months? Years?
•How would your life look different now?
•How would this change in direction have affected other people in your life?

Plot 20

You are a passenger on a cruise ship. The ship leaves port with everything as it should be. Six weeks later she arrives late to her destination with half of her passengers and crew, none of her cargo, and a mysterious child that no one will claim. Tell the story of what happened through weekly journal entries.

Plot 21

A) Write down five goals, five places, five objects, five people, and five special skills.

B) Cut them up and make five piles. Randomly select one item from each pile to make five groups of story elements.

C) For each group, write down five potential story problems that your character might have to face in meeting his or her goal.

Future Exercises: Plot 25

Plot 22

A) You have been appointed to help develop a social charter for Earth's first human colony on another planet. There will be only 300 people and limited resources. Life will be difficult in the beginning and survival will depend on each person doing their part and cooperating as a whole.

Brainstorm potential challenges that your colonists might face socially, psychologically, environmentally, etc.

B) Choose a challenge to focus on and consider how that one challenge might be turned into a specific story problem.

Plot 23

A) Use the following sentence as a prompt for at least one page of free writing:

The flowers were taller than I was.

B) After writing, consider the following questions:

•Did the story end up being about literal flowers?
•What emotional undertones came through in your writing?
•Is there a clear emotional arc to the piece, or does it zigzag or remain constant?
•How can emotion drive plot and vice versa?

Plot 24

Recall a vivid dream. Write it down from start to finish. Go back through and use your imagination create a coherent narrative.

Plot 25

A) Pull out the five story ideas that you generated in *Plot 21*. Select one and spend 10 minutes writing a very short story using each of the story elements (including one story problem) that you selected. Do not make an outline in advance.

B) Read back through your story and make an outline after the fact. Consider the following questions:

•How is this outline different from outlines that you've made in advance of writing?
•Do you prefer writing with or without an outline? Why?
•What did you learn from your post-write outline?

Voice

Voice 1

Writing About The Senses: Sound

A) Listen carefully to the sounds around you. Choose one to focus on. As you listen to this sound, write down as many adjectives as you can think of to describe the experience.

B) For every word you wrote down, write two synonyms.

C) Listen again. Go back through your list and for each quality, circle the word that best fits the sensation. Examine your results. Consider the following:

•How many times did you choose to keep the first word you wrote down?
•How many times did you choose a synonym over your original word?
•What did you learn from this?

Voice 2

Write a personal reflection about your favorite story. Consider the following questions as you write:

•What did you like about it?
•In what context did you first experience this story?
•What elements from this story can be found in other stories you like?
•Do you tend to incorporate similar elements in your own writing?

Voice 3

What if individual automobiles were outlawed?

Future Exercises: Voice 9

Voice 4

If you could travel in time, when would you visit? What would you do there? Why?

Future Exercises: Voice 18

Voice 5

A) Free-write the first page of a story in any genre or topic you wish. Say the story aloud as you write.

B) After you finish, go back and read through your writing. Consider the following questions:

•Does this story read in generally the same way as your other work, or did writing aloud affect your style?
•Did you find it helpful to write aloud? Why or why not?
•Did writing aloud affect how the story unfolded?
•Did writing aloud affect which details you included?
•Did writing aloud make it harder or easier to turn off your inner editor as you wrote?

Voice 6

Write down something that happened to you yesterday. It can be an everyday occurrence or something out of the ordinary.

Voice 7

What do you want to accomplish in the next 12 months? What steps do you need to take to get there? What challenges do you see? How might you overcome them?

Voice 8

Writing About The Senses: Smell

A) Find something safe to smell. As you breathe in the scent, write down as many adjectives as you can think of to describe the experience. Think deeply. Consider flavors, effects on your mood, etc.

B) For every word you wrote down, find two synonyms.

C) Smell the object again. Go back through your list and for each quality, circle the word that best fits the sensation. Examine your results. Consider the following:

•How many times did you choose to keep the first word you wrote down?
•How many times did you choose a synonym over your original word?
•What did you learn from this?

Voice 9

A) Bring out your work from *Voice 1*. Take a moment to read back through it. Respond to the following prompts:

•As you responded to the original prompt, what did you focus on (for example, did you approach the question from more of an individual, societal, or environmental standpoint?)
•Were you aware of any particular focus when you wrote?
•Does anything about your writing surprise you now that you look back at it?

B) Now go through your piece and highlight each of the adjectives that you chose.

•How many did you use?
•Are there places where more or fewer adjectives might strengthen the piece? Why or Why not?
•How does this set of adjectives contribute to the emotional tone?

Voice 10

Words have the power to evoke emotions. What makes you smile when no-one is around? What makes you cry? What makes you want to reach out to others, to be yourself, to withdraw, to speak, or to stay silent?

Choose an emotion that you feel like exploring and do a one page free-write discussing the emotion that you chose. You might consider the following:

•What people, places, or events make you feel this emotion?
•How does this feeling affect your thoughts and behaviors?
•If you were to write a scene in which a character is experiencing this feeling, what kinds of words might you use?

Voice 11

New technology has made it suddenly possible to send colonies of people to other planets. Recruitment has been opened, and you are qualified to apply. Thinking realistically, would you be willing to leave Earth on a one-way journey to colonize a new planet? Answer the following questions as you consider your answer:

•How would you feel about leaving your home?
•How would you feel about staying behind while others left for the stars?
•Would it make a difference if friends or family were going? How so?
•What conditions would you need to find on the new planet in order to be comfortable physically? Socially? Psychologically?
•What other questions might you consider in making your decision?

Future Exercises: Voice 16

Voice 12

Choose a topic on which you have particularly strong feelings. Write a dialogue between two characters arguing the pros and cons of the issue.

Voice 13

Why do you think that humans are so prolific when it comes to making stories? Consider the following as you write:

•What do stories do for us individually? Socially? Culturally?

•How has story telling changed over time?

•How has it stayed the same?

•What is the difference between individual and shared storytelling?

•What are some ways in which humans have assigned value to storytelling?

•What are some ways in which humans have decried storytelling?

Voice 14

What is something new that you learned today? If you can't think of anything, what would you like to learn? What will you/would you do with this new information or skill?

Voice 15

What if you could literally 'relive' the past? Consider the following questions as you write:

•If you could travel back in time and resume life in the body of your former self, when would you travel to?
•Would you live as a child? A teenager? Just yesterday?
•What would you look forward to re-experiencing? Why?
•What would you not look forward to re-experiencing? Why?
•What would you do differently in your life if you had all of your current memories and experiences to take back with you?

Voice 16

Bring out your work from *Voice 11*. Did you decide to stay on Earth or head for the stars? Write a short scene from the point of view of a person who has chosen the opposite of what you chose. If you decided you would go, your character has chosen to stay behind. If you decided you would rather stay behind, your character has chosen to go. Either way, your scene takes place at the space port in which your character is either preparing to board the ship to leave Earth forever, or saying goodbye to the opportunity to go.

Voice 17

Take out a piece of writing you've worked on previously. Rewrite the piece in a different narrative voice. For example, if you originally wrote in the third person, change it to the first. Answer the following questions:

•Did changing the voice alter the flow of the activity?
•Did changing the voice make me feel closer to or farther from the characters?
•Which voice did you prefer as a writer? Why?
•Which voice do you prefer as a reader? Why?

Future Exercises: Voice 22

Voice 18

Review your writing from *Voice 4*. Write a scene from the point of view of a middle-aged man who has this ability.

Voice 19

Writing About The Senses: Taste

A) Find something safe to taste. Write down as many adjectives as you can think of to describe the experience. Think deeply. Consider bitter, sweet, salty, temperature, texture, emotional response, etc.

B) For every word you wrote down, find two synonyms.

C) Taste again. Go back through your list and for each quality, circle the word that best fits the sensation. Examine your results. Consider the following:

•How many times did you choose to keep the first word you wrote down?
•How many times did you choose a synonym over your original word?
•What did you learn from this?

Voice 20

A) Pull out a story that you have written in a previous prompt. Read through it. Using your thesaurus, replace all adjectives and adverbs. Maintain the meaning, but change the vocabulary.

B) Read through the story again. Consider the following:

•Do the new word choices change the tone of the story?
•Do the new word choices change the readers understanding of the characters?
•Did trying different words enhance your own experience with the story? If yes, how so?
•After completing this exercise, what are your thoughts about word choice?

Voice 21

Writing About The Senses: Sight

A) Find something safe to look at. As you observe, write down as many adjectives as you can think of to describe the experience. Think deeply. Consider color, texture, angles, curves, etc.

B) For every word you wrote down, find two synonyms.

C) Look at the object again. Go back through your list and for each quality, circle the word that best fits the sensation. Examine your results. Consider the following:

•How many times did you choose to keep the first word you wrote down?
•How many times did you choose a synonym over your original word?
•What did you learn from this?

Voice 22

Take a moment to read both the original and revised versions of the writing you used for *Voice 17*. Answer the following questions:

•How did changing the voice affect the tone of the story?
•How might the change affect how close the reader feels to the character?
•Did you have to add new lines of text to make the story make sense in the new voice or were the changes fairly minimal?
•What were the strengths and weaknesses of the piece for each voice you used?

Voice 23

If you knew you were going to live forever, what would you do differently today? How might your life goals shift? What would you want to do for the next decade? Century? Millennia?

Voice 24

Writing About The Senses: Touch

A) Find something safe to touch. As you feel the object, write down as many adjectives as you can think of to describe the experience. Think deeply. Consider texture, temperature, hardness, shape, etc.

B) For every word you wrote down, find two synonyms.

C) Touch the object again. Go back through your list and for each quality, circle the word that best fits the sensation. Examine your results. Consider the following:

•How many times did you choose to keep the first word you wrote down?
•How many times did you choose a synonym over your original word?
•What did you learn from this?

Voice 25

Add a fantastical element to the world around you. For example, perhaps animals can talk, lovers can read minds, or people can travel to new places simply by thinking about them. Write about the effects this element might have on your daily life. Some things to consider as you write might include:

•How would this element affect my goals in life?
•How would this element affect the way that I reach my goals?
•How would this element affect my family, social, and work relationships?
•How would this element affect government policies, laws, and security measures?
•How would this element affect religious and spiritual practices?